MULTIPLE EARNINGS FROM EBOOK CREATION AND PUBLISHING

Dr.Friday Ojeaburu

Copyright © 2021 Friday Ojeaburu

All rights reserved

The characters and events portrayed in this book are fictitious. Any similarity to real persons, living or dead, is coincidental and not intended by the author.

No part of this book may be reproduced, or stored in a retrieval system, or transmitted in any form or by any means, electronic, mechanical, photocopying, recording, recording, scanning, lithography or unauthorized printings by any person or entity are strictly forbidden and must obtain permission of the copyright owner.

ISBN-13: 9798468516379

Cover design by: Art Painter
Library of Congress Control Number: 2018675309
Printed in the United States of America

This book is dedicated to God Almighty for his love and my family for their support

CONTENTS

Title Page
Copyright
Dedication
Introduction
CHAPTER ONE   1
CHAPTER TWO   3
CHAPTER THREE   5
CHAPTER FOUR   7
CHAPTER FIVE   10
CHAPTER SIX   13
CHAPTER SEVEN   15
About The Author   17

INTRODUCTION

Master eBooks creation and publishing guide are essential to get acquitted with it. This generation is a knowledge era where one convert knowledge into wealth. This eBook covers how to sign up, how to create eBooks and paperback. It also covers values systems, multiple sources of earnings and client management. I strongly recommend this eBook for life transformation and capacity development.

CHAPTER ONE

VALUE SYSTEM

Because you need more information then you have to follow all instructions to get what you want. The bedrock of the master class and the mind of someone that wants to excel in life is to follow instruction. The only success rule is to follow instructions, follow your coach or your leader, only submit when you are asked to submit, do not send message to coach or leader but only when you are asked to do so, do not ask your coach or leader questions privately but wait until you asked to do so, and always take time to find out where you need to submit particular information.

Information is the highest and largest wealth mine on the earth. This master class training I have received has shown me how to transfer rich knowledge to the younger generations. So as a learner, be opened hearted. Remember you have a value system that needs to be an overhaul. You need to drop something in life and go for information that will change the course of your future. Asking for material or information already shared; drawing back or asking to repeat what was well delivered. If you always complain and give an excuse, it can make you stunted and redundant. To avoid redundancy and stunted growth by avoiding complain and giving excuses. Ignorant; poverty; suppression; oppression must give way for one to have a good value system.

Now, we are in the information age. Information is money. Information is wealth. The likes of Jeff, Bill Gate, Dangote, Adenuga are where they are today because of how they turn every information they have to wealth. The richest companies in the world operate in digitally. Companies like Paypal, Alibaba, Google, Yahoo, Facebook and Amazon depend on digital. That digital came with information. It is relevant that you go for where you can get information. This is the crux of the matter, which make training a relevant source every aspiring billionaire must go for.

CHAPTER TWO

10 RELEVANT OF MASTER CLASS EBOOK TRAINING

A Master class eBook training has made so many followers start earnings from multiple sources. Training is a necessity for growth and development. During the period of training, one will be guided on how to use the Amazon App. Once the Amazon App is downloaded into your computer, the next thing is to format your manuscripts. This single task will launch you into earning from multiple sources. The training will make you learn the advanced method of eBook creation and publishing that will unlock so many opportunities. The Amazon App is the same as the kindle create app/software. Below are ten relevant master class eBook creation and publishing of this eBook.

1. Undergoes this training will open the door for one to make money. Regina Kingola (MC11) struck a deal of $500 under a month after graduation to write a book. It is true that you start earning after graduation and afterwards. This kind of earnings is different from the one from royalty in Amazon or other publishers.

2. The training will empower you to start earning royalty from your eBooks and paperback from Amazon. Olu Ogunlade (MC15) send evidence of $3.40 royalties received from one of the eBooks published. Arc Solomon Okpa showed us during the training screenshot of some of his eBook Royalty of $3.48 earned from Amazon.

3. The training will make one self-reliant. According to o Dr Awosusi (MC) when he counselled another MC, Alaukwe Nne that

the essence of the practical aspect of the training was to make students self-reliant.

4. The training will equip and empower you for your consultancy job ahead. Arc Solomon Okpa gave an instance where they also go consultancy job.

5. The training will make one exudes massive confidence. This was extracted from Regina Kingola (MC11), her letter of appreciation to Ogapatapata of Write-For-Me.

6. The training will give you an edge over other applicants. Mgbemere Akudo Anastasia (MC1) supported that when she said the MC training had given her an edge over others. She was the best graduating student of August/September Master's eBook training in 2020.

7. The training will allow you to be an affiliate of WRITE-FOR-ME. It is optional

8. The knowledge of this kindle creat app will bring you gold money. Ogapatapata stated this in the cause of the training we had with him.

9. The training will make you acquire a skill set. Skillset means the abilities, qualities and experiences students require to perform well. Dan Lok record showed as one of the best copywriters in the world. This guy is one of the Ogapatapata mentors.

10. The training will equip you to be able to train others. You can gain their attention by showing them the eBooks you have published. Monetization can reward you more.

CHAPTER THREE

FAILURES AN OPPORTUNITIES

Anything a billionaire fails, he wants to know why he fails to make amend. Failure is an opportunity for more doors. Failure and success are both decisions. The group that see failures as a downfall are the poor. As you are about to join a race, you join to win. That is the goal. A goal helps one to know where he or she is going to be in the future. There are three goals of a master's class such as skill acquisition, certification and monetization. You are to decide what will be your goal based on the grades distinction, merit, credit and participant. Instead for they to endure the situation like the USA, China, Japan, Europe that were built and endured challenges. Look at these instances and how they all responded to the situation they find themselves in.

1. Student targeting Credit Grades: Even as most students are having distinction in view, some are targeting credit from the filling of the first form before they are certified Master's eCreator. This is already a sign of failure. The expected grade of someone that wants to excel would have been a distinction, not even merit, not even credit and not even past.

2. Student that came up with Pass Grade: After the complaints by a student with the pass. A former registrar, Dr Awosusi who gave the validation speech during their convocations told her to thank God for completing this course successfully. That pass grade is the same in the university system but cannot limit your success in life making an instance of some SAN, Governors, and senators that came out with pass but today they are well placed in the society. He concluded that a grade is evidence of completion not the controller of the future. He also stated that the assessment criteria are in order, just that students don't follow instructions and when Ogapatapata was mentoring the things that could reduce or enhance their scores.

3. **Student that came out with Participant Grade:** This student had heartbroken lamentations. She stated that she did all that was asked to do including the project of training basic class students but still come out as a participant. The guidelines started before joining the training that they only grade performance not attendance. It is because the student did not follow the instruction as the bedrock of this training. The rich look at performance, not attendance or participation. One can participate with value addition.

CHAPTER FOUR

TOOLS TO SUCCESS

Some say one of the tools to success is knowledge. How much of the knowledge will determine how much you can make in life. So, first, to start earning from multiple sources in eBooks creation and publishing, they are certain criteria everyone is supposed to pass like get registered to create a kdp account. EBooks are electronics or digital books while paperback are hard copies or physical books. Follow this process and get register to start enjoying the usage of this amazing App.

OPERATION OF KDP ACCOUNT

1. You will need to create or continue with your existing kdp.amazon.com account and set up the two-step verification. For the account to be secure you need to either enable SMS or email to receive OTP.
2. The next is to complete the form. The form contains your details, tax information etc that must be properly filled to have your account showing "complete"
3. You will in your account know how to publish your eBook & paperback in a basic way.
4. You will know how to create your eBook and paperback covers respectively.
5. In the account, you will also find how to complete a description of your book, keywords, categories for your publication
7. You find the sense and essence of this master's class training - USING THE KINDLE CREATE APP/SOFTWARE to format your manuscripts. This is where so many people get confused. The Quintessential award of one of the previous sessions went to a student for giving accurate responses.

8. The next thing is Master's eBook Creation and Publishing. You must master the tool to work. Being a master will give an edge over certain things.

CREATION OF BASIC EBOOK AND PAPERBACK
You will be able to create a new title, manage the series and create free ISBN all by yourself at the comfort of your home without any support from a consultant. During the process of creation, you will be required to fill in the title of your book, the subtitle, the series and edition, the description, keywords and own the copyright by clicking the appropriate box before you click to submit to continue.

On the next page, you will be required to create a free ISBN and create a cover or you upload from the free cover pages from Amazon. You need to generate free ISBN for only your paperback but eBooks do not require ISBN. The information in your eBooks can only be edited during and after publishing, except the author's name and book title because the ISBN allocated to them is permanent.

You will know where to find the digital right management that make it impossible for people to download your eBooks and paperback. The option to enable or disable is also clear.

The last page dealt with pricing. The pricing must not be below $2.99 to charge for your eBooks or paperback. Before the pricing, is expected you carry our survey of price in the market about your proposed eBook to ensure your price is not at the high size.

After saving your eBook publishing, it could be seen as a draft. Draft means some issues need to be resolved. The problem could stem from your manuscript upload or cover. It can also be a mismatch from iSBN or when you fail to preview before publishing. The remedy is to quickly check through what you have done to possibly sport the issues and resolve them.

UNDERSTANDING KDP ACCOUNT.

In the account, you can also find reports, community and marketing. In the report section, you will view all your report to see your performance. You will be able to see the sales dashboard, payments, pre-orders, promotions etc under your report.

In the community section, you can join any of the community to inquiry or contribute to any discussions. Forum topics such account-one can post questions related to your KDP account setup; bookshelf-one can post questions related to your KDP bookshelf and title status; feedback-one can post feedbacks related to your KDP publishing experience; formatting-one can post questions related to formatting your book; general questions-one can post general publishing questions; kindle vella-one can post questions related Kindle Vella; payment-one can post questions related to setting up and receiving payments; reports-one can post questions related to royalty reporting, and voice of the author/ publisher-one can post feedback on features you'd like to see from KDP.

CHAPTER FIVE

KINDLE CREATE APP IS GOLD MONEY

Kindle create app is a way to earn gold money or digital money. You could have goods eBooks that have come alive but not selling. The reason could be because the formatting is not good enough for Amazon to put on sales. Amazon introduced a kindle create App to replace the old format of formatting. Don't just upload your manuscripts on the app and next proceed to publish. The first thing you need to do before you commence formatting with the app is to generate your iSBN. Use this iSBN generated to replace the iSBN in the kindle create an app.

Your kindle create app can reject formatting only when your iSBN, name and title doesn't match with what you imputed in your kdp account and the allocated iSBN.

Your manuscript must follow this step before you are supposed to publish your eBook.

- Research and prepare your manuscript
- Format the manuscript with the help of Kindle create App
- Publish the eBook and paperback and ensure both are linked together.

The manuscripts you intend to format on the kindle create app should start from chapter I to the last chapter excluding title page, copyright page etc. But the excluded pages will later be added to the formatting and preview to ensure completeness and correctness of the manuscript before publishing.

LINK FOREIGN BANK ACCOUNT

The first is to open your bank account with Payoneer from the comfort of your home. Go through the Payoneer website to sign up for an account. Fill all forms and provide all the necessary information need to open an account. In the process of opening the account, you should use a proper address, valid local bank account number, valid identity card and valid phone number. The focus now shows to be creating the account not withdrawal from the account. You could get blocked if your information is inconsistent or invalid. Please note, that your Payoneer account is a typical bank account. Once your request is approved, you are automatically assigned a US-based bank account with details.

Immediately your account is created, an account will be allocated a unique bank account number which you can use to link your account in kdp.amazon.com. After your account has been created and approved, check the homepage and click on receiving. Ensure you select only USA instead of adding both USA and UK together to avoid challenges in the future. Copy the bank details and paste them into the section of kdp amazon.com account to merge the account. Take your time and don't rush to copy and paste all the information correctly. Through this means, you will have your money paid to you. The system allowed you to apply for a free debit card that can be used in ATMs which is an option. You can cash out from your local bank.

You are to ensure your name in Payoneer is the same as the name in kdp account to avoid conflict. Because some marketplaces requested that you list the name registered with Amazon as the beneficiary name to receive the earnings. The Payoneer account can also be used to receive money from other sources. Please read their terms and conditions for more information on that.

PROJECTING YOUR EBOOKS TO THE WORLD
It is one thing to produce eBooks and it is another thing to promote, market and sell it to the right customers and audiences. Here, we look at digital marketing. The cheapest among the strategies is the advert, promote and marketing done by you either

through word-of-mouth or through social media like Facebook, Twitter, medium etc.

You may also engage kdp for their paid marketing plans and also digital marketers to ensure that your eBooks are spread all over the world. That can boost your earnings.

CHAPTER SIX

TESTIMONIES OF PREVIOUS MASTER'S eCREATORS

The most passionate student of MC 16, Archibong Ukoh was a 72 years old man. To be successful, one must drop some old ways like age; title; financial statement, status. The previous training received the high calibre of an individual like VC, a student from America War College, politicians and men with locally and internationally influenced. A selected list of those previous master eCreators who are already making progress in the world of contact is measured below:

1. Eucharia Ezigbo who was the most industrious student in the MC10 set gave candid advice during her graduation. That person should stop complaining, not to hinder their progress. Don't waste your time on unnecessary things instead see when challenges as a stepping stone. Everyone should be able to rate his or her performance at the end of every contest. She demonstrated a level of confidence in the management of WRITE-FOR-ME.

2. Dr Safuya Tanko and Dr Elizabeth Ajila both gave instances where they could not utilize the devices in their possession but with the training received from Write-For-Me, they can now use them.

3. Stephen Yakubu(MC14) have agreed with the common saying that truth is bitter. This was stated in the testimony title 'The Truth: A bitter Pill'. This was because he had patiently listened and sacrificed his time to the class till the end. He thanks Ogapatapata for emerging his spirit. He stated that he got offended for his frantic talk and expressions, which got him pissed up at a time. But he

reluctantly moved on until he saw the usefulness of the class and concluded that nothing indeed comes easy in life.

4. Mrs Ify Evangel Obim (MC8) a University lecturer, who is the best graduating student in MC8 gave a testimony that success is about determination, vision and focus.

5. Glory Omowunmi Alaska was the most industrious student of MC13 and graduated with distinction. Master's Class is a great blessing. I now own a laptop. After receiving the required skills, she introduced her husband and daughter to MC 14. The Master Class conquered a whole family.

6. MC Anthonia Lola Dickson gave testimony for being able to publish her eBooks by herself. That immediately the eBook is published she started receiving the order. Her word *'I published just within a few hours. You will not believe sir, people have started buying the book'*.

CHAPTER SEVEN

CLIENTS MANAGEMENT

In this business of eBooks creation and publishing, there will be a time when consultants have many clients to manage. For there to be client management, there must be a contract. The contract is very key in the writing and publishing business. The contract can be just an exchange of correspondence, with the captions: please reply if these prices are ok by you or make payment of the certain amounts (figure) to start. Make it simple as possible. The contract can also be informed of coming together physically to endorse. In this case, you are expected to print, sign and scan back the signatory pages. All that is done must be detailed and professional to checkmate dubious clients.

This is another key multiple source of earnings that must be taken likely. A professor friend of mine does not know to publish on Amazon and other publishing platforms. Imagine where you have a professor at his level of education who does not how to self-publish to earn money. What is required is to develop the market and in a short while the money starts rolling into your bank account.

Certain things to do when publishing for your client; ensure all the requirements to open kdp account and Payoneer account are met and accurately filled; use the client's name during registration but use a special email address open for the purpose; the special email address will enable you to have firsthand information and commutations to avoid contacting your clients for such information.

Your client could be charged based on the following factors as

follow:
- Account opening
- eBooks publishing
- paperback publishing
- the volume of the manuscripts
- the contents of the manuscripts
- the client financial muscles
- Training of the client
- annual monitoring fee
- other factors that can impact the cost.

After the conclusion of the contract, the consultant could hand it over to his or her client by changing the email address to the clients own email address and give the client operational guidelines to enable him to achieve effective monitoring of the account.

ABOUT THE AUTHOR

Friday Ojeaburu

Ojeaburu Friday is a seasoned Chartered Accountant and holds a Bachelor of Science (BSc) Degree in Accountancy and Finance from Ambrose Ali University, Master of Science (MSc) Degree in Accounting from University of Port Harcourt and PhD Degree in Financial Accounting from Ignatius Ajuru University of Education, Port Harcourt, Rivers State. He is a full member of both the Institute of Chartered Accountants of Nigeria (ICAN) and Associate member of Nigerian Accounting Association(ANAA) with substantial experience in both the private and public sector spanning over 14 years in financial management, audit & investigation, public sector accounting, environmental accounting, entrepreneurial accounting. career development and online coaching and mentorship etc.

www.ingramcontent.com/pod-product-compliance
Lightning Source LLC
Chambersburg PA
CBHW030046230526
45472CB00005B/1706